WHAT SHOULD I
Do with My Guilt?

The Crucial Questions Series By R.C. Sproul

Who Is Jesus?

Can I Trust the Bible?

Does Prayer Change Things?

Can I Know God's Will?

How Should I Live in This World?

What Does It Mean to Be Born Again?

Can I Be Sure I'm Saved?

What Is Faith?

What Can I Do with My Guilt?

What Is the Trinity?

What Is Baptism?

Can I Have Joy in My Life?

Who Is the Holy Spirit?

Does God Control Everything?

How Can I Develop a Christian Conscience?

What Is the Lord's Supper?

What Is the Church?

What Is Repentance?

What Is the Relationship between Church and State?

Are These the Last Days?

What Is the Great Commission?

Can I Lose My Salvation?

Free digital editions available at ReformationTrust.com/FreeCQ

CRUCIAL
QUESTIONS
No. | 9

WHAT CAN I
Do with
MY GUILT?

R.C. SPROUL

ℝ *Reformation Trust*   A DIVISION OF LIGONIER MINISTRIES, ORLANDO, FL

What Can I Do with My Guilt?

© 2011 by R.C. Sproul

Published by Reformation Trust Publishing
a division of Ligonier Ministries
421 Ligonier Court, Sanford, FL 32771
Ligonier.org   ReformationTrust.com

Printed in North Mankato, MN
Corporate Graphics
August 2015
First edition, sixth printing

Cover design: Gearbox Studios
Interior design and typeset: Katherine Lloyd, The DESK

All Scripture quotations are from *The Holy Bible, English Standard Version*®, copyright © 2001 by Crossway Bibles, a publishing ministry of Good News Publishers. Used by permission. All rights reserved.

Library of Congress Cataloging-in-Publication Data

Sproul, R. C. (Robert Charles), 1939-
  What can I do with my guilt? / R.C. Sproul.
     p. cm. -- (The crucial questions series)
  ISBN 978-1-56769-258-7
  1. Guilt--Religious aspects--Christianity. 2. Forgiveness--Religious aspects--Christianity. I. Title. II. Series.
  BT722.S67 2011
  234'.5--dc22

                                        2011014993

Contents

Chapter One

GUILT AND
GUILT FEELINGS

During my career as a seminary professor, I frequently
have been called upon to teach courses on Christian
apologetics. The term *apologetics* comes from the Greek word
apologia, which means "to make a reply." Thus, the discipline
of apologetics is not concerned with apologizing for being
a Christian, as the term might suggest. Rather, its aim is to
provide a rational, intellectual defense of the truth claims of
Christianity and to answer objections that people raise to the
faith. This can be a very abstract, philosophical enterprise.

As I engage in apologetics, I often converse with people who are not Christian believers; some of them are indifferent, while others are openly hostile to Christianity. For this reason, when I have these discussions, I often encounter questions about various truth claims. I think, as Francis Schaeffer used to say, that it is the Christian responsibility to give honest answers to honest questions, as far as we are able, so I try my best to do that.

Sooner or later, however, particularly in discussions with skeptics and people who are philosophically hostile to Christianity, I pause from my attempts to give answers and raise a particularly pointed question of my own. I say: "We've discussed the abstractions, the rational arguments for the existence of God and so on. Let's lay those aside just for a moment and let me ask you this: What do you do with your guilt?"

This question often provokes a dramatic shift in the tenor of the discussion. It touches on something that is a visceral matter for many people, something that affects them at an existential level, so it moves the discussion beyond the abstract realm. In most instances, the person with whom I am speaking does not become angry when I ask this question. Sometimes the person will say that he has no guilt or that guilt is simply a term invented by religious people. Usually, however, the person treats the question seriously and tries to explain how he is dealing with guilt. This, I think, is evidence that every human being knows what guilt is. Every human being, at some level and at some point in his or her life, has to deal with it.

GUILT: AN OBJECTIVE REALITY

What is guilt? In the first place, we have to say that guilt is not subjective but objective because it corresponds to an objective standard or reality. That leads me to the simplest definition of guilt that I can compose: Guilt is that which a person incurs when he violates a law.

We understand how this works in the criminal justice system. If someone breaks a law, a statute that has been enacted by a government, and that person is apprehended for having broken the law, he may have to appear in court. The person may say he is not guilty, in which case he is entitled to a trial, frequently a trial by jury. At such a trial, evidence is produced and testimony is heard. At the end of the trial, the members of the jury come to a verdict. They decide whether, in their judgment, the person is, in fact, guilty of breaking the law he is charged with violating.

There is a wide range of kinds of trials, kinds of arguments that are used, and levels of evidence. Some years ago, it seemed that the entire United States was transfixed by the two trials of O. J. Simpson—one a criminal trial, the other a civil trial—which featured different rules on evidence, different guidelines for reaching a verdict, and so forth. But in any kind of trial, the key question is this: Is the person guilty? In other words, did the suspect do it? Did he or she transgress the law?

Laws are an inescapable reality in our world. There are rules imposed by our parents. There are rules imposed by teachers and by employers. There are laws enacted by the states and the federal government. All of us are subject to rules and laws. We might disagree with some of these laws or even with the idea of laws altogether. We might not have had the opportunity to vote on the laws we are required to heed. Still, those laws are there. We cannot ignore them. When we talk about guilt, we're talking about the transgression or violation of these rules or laws.

The biblical view is that God is the supreme Lawgiver and that He holds every person who is alive accountable for conforming to His mandates. Yes, God has rules and laws. People have said to me on many occasions that Christianity is not about rules and regulations; it's about love. That's simply not true. Christianity is about love, but that is because love is one of the rules—God commands us to love Him and to love one another. Christianity is not just about rules and laws, but rules and laws decreed by God have been a fact of life since the day of creation. So if we define guilt as that which a person incurs when he violates a law, we incur supreme guilt when we break the law of God. That is because His law is perfect. It is never arbitrary. It does not reflect merely the vested interests of a particular lobby group, but the perfect, holy, righteous character of God Himself.

Obviously, if there is no God, we don't have to worry about breaking His rules, because He doesn't have any rules. Still, we have the rules of the lesser magistrates to deal with. I believe all of us have broken the law of God, but even if we have not violated God's laws, we've certainly broken the laws of men. So all of us have experienced the objective situation of having transgressed a law.

Suppose a person commits murder with malice afore-thought; he willfully plans to take another person's life, then executes his plan. The vast majority of people in this world agree that killing is a bad thing, that murder is wrong. Even in this age of relativism, when many people say there are no absolutes, a person will fudge on his commitment to relativism if someone comes at him with a knife and threatens to kill him. He will say, "That's wrong, and if you kill me maliciously, you will incur guilt." He's right. At some level, we all understand that there are certain things that are inherently wrong, and if we do those things, we incur guilt.

GUILT FEELINGS: A SUBJECTIVE RESPONSE

An interesting thing occurs when I ask people, "What do you do with your guilt?" I don't ask what the person is going to do about his or her guilt *feelings*. My question has to do with his or her guilt. However, almost everyone to whom I pose this question tends to respond concerning his or her guilt feelings. At that point, I stop the discussion to make a careful distinction between guilt and guilt feelings. While these two are closely related, they are not precisely the same thing. The basic distinction is between objectivity and subjectivity.

Let's think about feelings for a moment. Feelings are things that personal beings experience. Rocks, to our knowledge, do not experience personal feelings. They are cold, lifeless objects. Therefore, if someone throws a stone and it hits me in the head, the person who threw the stone may or may not experience guilt, but I can safely conclude that the stone suffers no trauma of psychological import. The stone is the instrument that is used in this particular assault, but it doesn't have feelings. People are different. People are personal beings. They have minds and wills. Each of them has a feeling aspect in his or her life. So when we talk about guilt feelings, we're talking about something that is personal and subjective.

Guilt without guilt feelings. As we seek to sort out the differences between guilt and guilt feelings, it is important to remember that our feelings do not always have a perfect correspondence to our status under the law. A pair of examples will help make this clear.

We have an expression for people who cannot be deterred from parking in no-parking zones. They get tickets for it and simply throw them in the garbage can, or they get summonses to pay or appear in court but simply ignore them. We call them "scofflaws." They seem able to repeat their habit of violating no-parking zones without any sense of personal remorse.

Taking this idea to a higher level, in the study of psychology, there is a category of people who are called psychopaths or sociopaths. The common element of these two terms is the suffix *path*; it comes from the Greek term *pathos*, which means "suffering, feeling, emotion." A psychopath or a sociopath is a person who can commit antisocial behavior, such as a heinous crime, with no apparent feeling of remorse. Sometimes it is said that a person is a psychopathic liar. This means that the person not only lies habitually and consistently, but does so without suffering any particular assaults from his conscience.

When people commit terrible crimes without feeling guilty, their feelings are not proportionate to the guilt that they have actually incurred. So, it is possible for people to have guilt without guilt feelings, or at least without proportionate guilt feelings. The lack of guilt feelings does not always indicate a lack of guilt.

Imagine that someone is arrested for murder in the first degree, and the prosecution has audio and videotapes of the person declaring in advance his hostility toward the victim and his firm intent to murder the person. There is also video of the actual murder, DNA evidence, and even the murder weapon. However, the person comes into court and, when the judge asks, "How do you plead?" he says, "I plead not guilty." He then elects to defend himself rather than use an attorney. He stands before the court and mounts his defense, saying: "I am not guilty because I don't feel guilty. Never mind all the objective evidence. My subjective testimony establishes my innocence. I can't be guilty because I don't feel guilty." How far do you think that defense would go in a secular courtroom? The fact that a person says he is not guilty because he does not feel guilty does not establish his innocence, because the mere fact that a person does not feel guilty says absolutely nothing about whether he actually broke the law regarding murder.

It is possible for people not to feel even the guilt they bear before God. In the third chapter of the book of Jeremiah, the prophet speaks of the infidelity of the people of God in the Old Testament. As is often the case in the Bible, Israel's unfaithfulness is described by use of the metaphor of adultery—Israel is seen as a harlot who has joined herself to foreign deities. Jeremiah writes:

> "If a man divorces his wife and she goes from him and becomes another man's wife, will he return to her? Would not that land be greatly polluted? You

have played the whore with many lovers; and would you return to me? declares the LORD. Lift up your eyes to the bare heights, and see! Where have you not been ravished? By the waysides you have sat awaiting lovers like an Arab in the wilderness. You have polluted the land with your vile whoredom. Therefore the showers have been withheld, and the spring rain has not come; yet you have the forehead of a whore; you refuse to be ashamed." (3:1–3)

Jeremiah's imagery here is quite graphic. In voicing God's judgment against Israel, he accuses Israel of committing harlotry and describes Israel as having a harlot's forehead. What does that mean? Jeremiah is saying that Israel has forgotten how to blush. She is so practiced and habitual in her infidelity, she has lost any sense of embarrassment or shame.

Scriptural passages like this make it clear that there is often a large gap between objective guilt and the ensuing guilt feelings that flow from it. We are told in Scripture that it is possible for people, by repeated sins, to lose the capacity for embarrassment and shame. The Bible frequently speaks of the hardened heart, which causes a person no longer to feel remorse for his or her transgression. It is dangerous for us to rely totally on our guilt feelings to reveal to us the reality of our guilt itself because we can quench the pangs of conscience.

Guilt feelings without guilt. On the other hand, there are people who are plagued by all sorts of feelings of guilt for things they did not do. Objectively, they violated no laws, but because of one mental aberration or another, they feel guilty; they feel that they have violated a law or laws.

It is possible for people to feel guilty about things that, considered in and of themselves, are not sinful. Suppose, for example, you are raised in a Christian home that is part of a Christian subculture that teaches that this or that behavior is wicked. Your parents, teachers, and authority figures in the church drum into you that Christians are not allowed to do various things. In some cases, these rules and regulations are not found in Scripture. There is such a thing as legalism, which imposes laws where God has left men free. But whether they are truly sinful or not, you are taught that certain actions are against God's law, so if you do them, you incur a great sense of guilt. In short, you have guilt feelings, even though the behaviors you engage in are not under the judgment of God.

One common example of this concerns alcoholic beverages. Many people are taught that any consumption of alcoholic beverages is sinful. I do not believe the Bible teaches that. I am sure that I will get calls and letters from people who disagree with me, who have been taught in their churches or in their families that the wine of which the Bible speaks is merely unfermented grape juice. However, in ancient Israel, the religious festivals that were instituted by God, most notably the Passover, used real wine. It was a beverage that had the capacity, if overused or abused, to make people drunk. In Old Testament Israel, drunkenness was a problem, and God spoke against drunkenness and saw it as a serious sin. But the problem was the drunkenness, not the drink.

Likewise, the New Testament makes it clear that drunkenness is a sin. Nevertheless, Jesus made real wine at the wedding feast of Cana (John 2). *Oinos* is the Greek word that is translated as "wine," and it means the fermented fruit of the vine. Such wine was used for religious purposes, for daily dietary doses, and also in times of celebration. The Bible speaks of the wine that makes the heart glad (Ps. 104:15). When Jesus established the Lord's Supper, He consecrated real wine. Jesus was celebrating the Passover with His disciples when He instituted the Lord's Supper, and wine was used in the Passover celebration.

The common Christian teaching against alcoholic beverages grew out of Prohibition and the temperance movement in the United States. It has no foundation in the lexicography of the ancient languages. Nevertheless, many who are exposed to this teaching and then consume alcohol come away with feelings of guilt, even though they have committed no sin.

At the same time, the Bible tells us that whatever is not of faith is sin (Rom. 14:23). Let me illustrate this. I have a friend who loved to play Ping-Pong. Now the Bible doesn't say anything about playing Ping-Pong; Ping-Pong was not even invented at the time the Bible was written, and I think that we can readily see that there is no intrinsic evil in engaging in a simple pastime or recreational sport such as Ping-Pong. But even this simple activity can become an occasion for sin. My friend was an earnest Christian who had serious responsibilities at his job, but he became so caught up in Ping-Pong that he started to neglect his job, his family, and his other responsibilities. He was addicted to playing Ping-Pong. So for him, Ping-Pong became a moral issue, not because Ping-Pong in and of itself is evil, but because this activity had become an occasion for sin and for irresponsibility in his life. So he began to have to struggle with Ping-Pong.

Likewise, if you believe that taking a drink of wine is a sin, and you take a drink of wine, then you have sinned. In my judgment, the sin is not in drinking the wine, because if taking a taste of wine is a sin, then Jesus was a sinner, and He would not qualify to be the sinless Savior of His people. He would be the Lamb *with* a blemish rather than the Lamb *without* blemish (1 Peter 1:19). But the principle is that that which is done without faith is sin, and if you do something that you believe is wrong, then the sin that you have committed is in acting against your conscience. You have done something with the thought of transgressing, and to choose to do something that you believe is wrong, even if it is not wrong, is wrong.

With these examples, I hope you can see why it is very important for us to get a clear understanding of the relationship between guilt and guilt feelings. The presence of guilt feelings does not automatically indicate the presence of objective guilt with respect to a particular action, but it may represent the presence of the guilt of acting against one's conscience. The bottom line is that any time we experience feelings of guilt, we need to step back and ask ourselves as honestly as we possibly can, "Have I broken the law of God?"

Whenever we confuse guilt and guilt feelings, we open ourselves to several problems. For example, people may take advantage of our sensitivity to certain behavioral patterns and try to impose on us guilt feelings that are not appropriate for the actions we have done. One of the easiest ways to manipulate people is to heap some kind of guilt upon them in an effort to shame or embarrass them into doing what we want. There are people who have become masters at guilt manipulation. The process of guilt manipulation can be very destructive and devastating in human relationships.

But that's a small problem compared to the other side of the coin. We can become professionals at silencing the feelings of real guilt. We live in a culture that teaches us that guilt feelings are inherently destructive because they undermine a person's sense of self-esteem. Even in the realm of psychology today, we're told that there's something wrong about telling people that their behavior is sinful. Karl Menninger wrote a book a few years ago titled *Whatever Became of Sin?* The driving idea here is that we don't want to tell anyone that his behavior is wrong because we might make him feel guilty, and if he feels guilty, he may suffer some kind of psychological distress.

THE REALITY OF OUR GUILT

Let me return now to the question I use in my apologetics discussions: "What do you do with your guilt?" A clever attorney would recognize that there is a problem with this question. The problem is that I have not established that there is any guilt. My question presupposes that the person has guilt with which he needs to deal.

This question is something like the question, "Have you stopped beating your wife?" If a man answers that question by saying "Yes," he is admitting that he once beat his wife, and if he answers "No," he is saying that he's still beating his wife. No matter how he answers the question, he is admitting to some kind of guilt. The question is in an illegitimate form.

So if I say to you without knowing you, "What do you do with your guilt?" you have every right to respond to me by saying: "What guilt? You're assuming that I have guilt." That is true, but I can make that assumption based on my theological and biblical perspective. That's why, when I ask this question, I do not start by arguing that there is such a thing as guilt. I can assume that people understand the reality of guilt.

In Romans 3, the apostle Paul gives an elaborate exposition of the fallenness of the human race. He writes: "Now we know that whatever the law says it speaks to those who are under the law, so that every mouth may be stopped, and the whole world may be held accountable to God. For by works of the law no human being will be justified in his sight, since through the law comes knowledge of sin. . . . For there is no distinction: for all have sinned and fall short of the glory of God" (3:19–23). Manifestly and unambiguously, the Scriptures teach here not only the reality of human guilt but the universality of it. God has declared the whole world and every person in it to be guilty of breaking His law.

You may say that I'm begging the question again, simply declaring the universality of guilt by reading a passage from the New Testament. But the universality of human guilt is not just the testimony of Scripture; it is part of the folklore or natural wisdom of many cultures. In technical terms, this idea is known as the *jus gentium*, "the law of the nations," which is the universal testimony of people, not only those who read the Bible or are committed to a particular religion, to the universality of guilt.

Have you ever said, "Nobody's perfect"? Do you agree with that universal negative affirmation? How many people do you know who really believe they are perfect? I never have met a person outside the Christian church who told me that he or she was perfect. I have met people inside the Christian church who claimed to have been perfected and to live in a perfect state. I think that they were hopelessly deluded at that point, but I cannot say I never have met a person who said he was perfect now. But even such people admit to past imperfections, and I have yet to meet a human being who has looked me in the eye and said, "I have never done anything wrong in my life."

Now, there may be people who think that, and I would have to give special attention to those who do, but I'm going to cut the Gordian knot here and speak to those who are not in that situation, because they are the overwhelming majority of people. They know that they have broken the law of God. Again, Paul says, "All have sinned and fall short of the glory of God." The word *sin* in the New Testament in the Greek language, *harmartia*, literally means "to miss the mark." It was borrowed from the sport of archery. The bowmen of antiquity would practice very much as archers do today, with targets, and the targets had segments and bull's-eyes, so that the archer would aim his bow and try to reach a particular level of accuracy by putting his arrow on that mark. *Harmartia* was the word used in antiquity when the archer missed the bull's-eye and came short of a perfect score. But when it is carried over into the theological categories of the New Testament, we're not talking about shooting arrows at targets, we're talking about life. We're talking about reaching the standard of the perfection of God's law, and the Scriptures say that no one has hit the mark. Everyone falls short of the standard of righteousness, the standard of moral conduct that has been established by God Himself. Because that's the case, everyone in the world is guilty before God.

Therefore, I can cut to the chase in normal conversation and say to a person, "What do you do with your guilt?" I'm not talking about his or her guilt before a kindergarten teacher, before the local police officer, or before the traffic court. I'm talking about the person's guilt before God. The most frequent response to that question is this: "I don't really worry about it that much, because it's God's job to forgive." The hope is that since everyone is in the same boat, the Maker of the boat and the Captain of the boat will not be all that distressed by one more person in the boat. If nobody's perfect, certainly God is going to have to grade us on a curve. He will have to do what we do—adjust the standard lower so He can meet us where we are.

In a sense, those who give this answer know they are missing the target with their arrows, so instead of moving further away from the target, they begin to move closer to the target to make it easier to hit the bull's-eye. But it's one thing to adjust the sight on the bow or to reduce the distance to the target, and it's another thing to ask God to adjust His character. Remember, the law of God flows out of the character of God, and His laws are righteous because He is righteous. He will not adjust the law that reflects His perfection to accommodate you and me. As long as He doesn't adjust that law, we remain guilty before that law.

We know from the study of psychology that there is probably nothing more paralyzing to human action than unresolved guilt feelings. Such feelings paralyze people. That's why, when we are confronted with guilt feelings, we need to deal with them. Unfortunately, all too often, we attempt to deal with our guilt and guilt feelings by man-made methods. In the next chapter, I want to examine these methods before turning to God's prescription for guilt and guilt feelings in the final chapter.

Chapter Two

DEALİNG
WİTH GUİLT

When I was a young boy in elementary school, my teachers had rules and regulations. One of the rules was that we were not to chew gum in class. Another rule was that we were not to talk to our friends during class. When we broke these rules and were caught, we had to endure various forms of punishment, ranging from standing in the hall to staying after school to writing sentences. Sometimes a student had to write "I will not chew gum in class" a hundred times on the blackboard.

If the infraction was more severe, the student was sent to the principal's office, which was a formidable experience. The first time a student was sent there, he received a scolding from the principal and a minor punishment, such as staying after school. In addition, he had to put his name on a large paddle made of wood. If the student was sent to the principal again, the principal asked, "What's your name?" and if he found that student's name written on the paddle, the paddle was then applied to a certain part of the student's anatomy. So there was a simple system of crime and punishment at my elementary school, with an escalating pattern of punishment.

The typical criminal justice system also features many levels of punishment that may be imposed for the violation of laws, from a simple fine all the way up to the death penalty. One common form of punishment is incarceration. It is interesting that when a person is convicted of a crime and is sent to prison, upon his release it is sometimes said that he has "paid his debt to society." This simple statement encapsulates the idea that the concepts of crime and punishment are often understood in the metaphorical language of economics, of indebtedness. A debt, of course, is something that is owed and can be repaid.

When we wrestle with the question of what we do with our guilt, at least on the human level, we are asking how we can make up for our guilt. We want to know what we can do to set the scales of justice back on an even plane. In some cases, we can make restitution or endure certain punitive measures.

But what about our guilt before God? There are a number of subtle ways by which we attempt to deal with the objective reality of this guilt.

DENYING OUR GUILT

One of the things that we do to deal with this guilt is to deny it. That's the most common response of human beings to the intrusion of the upsetting and disturbing consciousness of having violated God's law. We try to deny it to other people and we try to deny it to ourselves.

What does denial look like? In dealing with their guilt before God, some people say, "I don't believe in God, I don't believe in His law, and I don't believe I have guilt in God's sight." Of course, unbelief in God does not mean He does not exist. Refusal to believe in His law does not mean that there is no law. Likewise, not caring about God's response to one's guilt does not make the guilt go away. The Scriptures teach us that God has published His law plainly, not by putting it on billboards or on national television, but by giving us a record of His moral law in the written Scriptures.

People often respond to that assertion by saying, "I've never read the Bible, so I can't be held accountable for the law of God written down there." However, the Scriptures say that God has published His moral law not only on the tablets of stone that were delivered from Mount Sinai by Moses and became part of the inscripturated Bible, He has written His law on the hearts of His creatures. This means that every human being has an innate sense of what is right and wrong. Simply put, God has published His law in a place that no one can miss—it's not in some obscure law book tucked away on a back shelf in a library on a secluded Ivy League campus; rather, it is in our hearts.

When the Bible speaks of the heart in this context, it obviously is referring to the idea of the conscience. The conscience bears witness to the publication of the law of God in our hearts. So whether we like it or even acknowledge it, we cannot change the reality that we have some grasp of what is right and what is wrong.

The philosopher Immanuel Kant tried to demonstrate this innate sense of right and wrong without appeals to the Bible or to religion. Instead, he appealed to human consciousness and the universality of what he called "the categorical imperative," a universal sense of "oughtness" that every moral creature possesses.

We all know that we have moral obligations that we have not fulfilled. I saw this truth demonstrated in my own life. When I was a small boy during World War II, my father was overseas fighting with the United States Army Air Corp. My mother and I would listen to the newscasts daily at noon and at six o'clock, and I hated those times of the day, because part of every newscast was a report on the latest casualties. The radio reports reminded me of the vulnerable situation my father was in. Even as a little boy, I had some understanding that my father might not come back alive from the war.

Because of that fear, I hated World War II, and that made me hate the whole concept of fighting. One time during the war, I went to my mother quite earnestly and told her that I wanted to write a letter to Adolf Hitler, Benito Mussolini, Joseph Stalin, Franklin Delano Roosevelt, and Winston Churchill, asking them to stop the war so my daddy could come home. It was plain to me that what they were doing was wrong. My mother assured me that my idea was a good one, but she also told me it wouldn't work. I asked: "But why do they need to hurt each other and kill each other? What good is there in that?" I was absolutely naive; I had no understanding of geopolitics or the causes of international conflicts. I was naively altruistic. I simply could not understand why human beings would settle their differences with violence.

When I got a little older, about ten or so, I heard the big boys at the drugstore talk about their sexual exploits with their girlfriends, and I thought that was the most disgusting thing I had ever heard. I couldn't believe those guys would be interested in those topics because they were not of any interest to me at age ten. I resolved that when I got to be fifteen or sixteen, I would not take any interest in these things. I didn't understand about adolescence, puberty, and other such matters when I was ten.

However, as I got older, I began to be involved in fist-fights. That is, I started to use violence as a means of settling differences—just like Hitler, Stalin, and the rest. When I grew older still, I experienced the allure of lust. As a result, I began to experience a crisis of self-esteem because of my initial ventures into certain kinds of sinful activity. I was uncomfortable. I was ashamed of myself. I was disappointed in myself. Because of that shame, my behavioral patterns changed. Not only that, my ethic, my moral expectations, not simply for other people but for myself, also changed. I adjusted my ideals downward. I adjusted my code of behavior downward. I adjusted my morality downward. Why? So that I could have an ethic I could live, a moral code that was within reach, one that would give my conscience rest and peace, and would leave me with a good feeling about myself instead of a rotten feeling. In essence, I was living in denial of my guilt. I am convinced that many people, if not all people, go through a similar process of denial.

It was not the Scriptures but Walt Disney who gave us the adage, "Let your conscience be your guide." This expression was uttered by Jiminy Cricket in the classic animated movie *Pinocchio*. We might call the idea behind this adage "Jiminy Cricket theology." There's a very real sense in which we are to act carefully according to the direction of this inner voice of God that we call "conscience." But we must remember that for us to be wise in following the dictates of our conscience, we must first make sure that our consciences are informed by the Word of God.

Thomas Aquinas once described the human conscience as that inner voice that either accuses or excuses us for our behavior. There are times when we sin and we feel the pangs of conscience, and the Holy Spirit works through our consciences to make us sensitive to our transgression against God, and there the conscience is doing what God created it to do. But as we saw in the previous chapter, the conscience can be seared. It can become immune to the accusation of the law of God. That's the judgment that God spoke to Israel when he said through the prophet Jeremiah, "You have the forehead of a whore."

RATIONALIZING OUR BEHAVIOR

If denial of our guilt before God doesn't work, the next step typically is to try to justify our behavior. We engage in rationalization, a spurious attempt to provide a sound, logical rationale for behavior that we know is wrong. Through rationalization, we seek to come up with an excuse for our immoral behavior.

Such excuses may be quite convincing, and they may be very effective in dealing with our friends or loved ones. They may even work to assuage the civil courts. However,

God tells us that His law calls every human being to account, "that every mouth may be stopped" (Rom. 3:19). What does this mean? The Scriptures uniformly describe the situation of the final judgment, when God gathers every human being before His tribunal, as one of silence. In human courts of law, we often hear the injunction, "Silence in the court." We observe a moment of silence when the judge comes in, but then the arguments begin as the lawyers start to set forth their cases. The Scriptures, however, say that the silence at the final judgment will be maintained. Every mouth will be stopped, because there will be no excuses, no denials, no protestations of innocence, no alibis. Paul tells us that we are without excuse when we violate the law of God (Rom. 1:20). In God's court, we're guilty, and nothing we can say can change it. It is absolutely futile for any human being to attempt to justify himself or herself before God.

Like denial, rationalization is designed to stifle or to quench the voice of the conscience. One of the reasons we do that is because guilt feelings are painful. There is an analogy, I think, between physical pain and psychological pain, the psychological pain that is associated with guilt feelings. Whenever a person experiences a stabbing pain, he is alarmed. He is uncomfortable because of it, so he seeks immediate relief. He might get painkillers to try to get rid of that uncomfortable feeling. Yet from a physical perspective, pain is an extremely important reality, because pain signals to us that there is something wrong, and if we cover up the pain, we could be covering up a life-threatening illness. Though we no longer suffer from the torment of the pain, we may be moving in a deadly direction.

By way of analogy, the pain that comes with guilt feelings is God's way of sending an alarm to our souls that speaks to us and tells us there is something wrong that we need to deal with. But we try to get relief from the pain by denying it or excusing it rather than understanding that guilt feelings may, and often do, have a therapeutic and redemptive importance to our lives.

COUNTING ON PAYMENT OR INDULGENCE

Some people do not bother to deny or rationalize their guilt. They simply assume that they'll come before God, admit their crimes, and then pay the penalty. They fail to distinguish between God's law and human law. Human law has provisions for making up for crimes through restitution, punishment, and so on. But how can we make up for a crime against God? How much time do we have to spend to make it right, to atone for offenses against an infinitely holy being? In the categories of biblical justice, our sins against God are infinitely heinous. That means we are unable to do the time. There is nothing we possibly could do to make up for our shortfall. That is why Jesus used the metaphor of the debtor who cannot pay his debts when He talked about forgiveness (Matt. 18:25).

Most people do not understand that the debt, the moral debt, we owe to God is so vast we never can repay it. So they say to themselves, "God is a God of love; He's a God of mercy; He will never require payment." They're hoping against hope that God will adjust His standards to meet them where they are, that He will give the human race a plenary indulgence and say: "Boys will be boys; girls will be girls. I'm not going to hold you personally accountable for your guilt." Many millions of people are counting on that. As a theologian, that terrifies me, because the Jesus who showed the world more than any living person ever the depths and riches of the love of God, the mercy of God, and the grace of God is the same Jesus who taught over and over again that there will be a final accounting, and that every idle word that you and I speak will be brought into the judgment.

As we have seen, we have real guilt before God. It's important for us to understand that nothing we can do—denying our guilt, rationalizing it away, attempting to make restitution, or blithely assuming that God will forgive it—can make our guilt before God go away.

Once, when I was in high school, I got into a fistfight with a student who was six feet seven inches tall, and I was never so happy to see the dean, because he broke up the fight and saved me. But the dean was not happy about this incident, and as a result of my violation of the school rules, I was given a three-day vacation from high school. That was a very serious matter in those days, because admission to college was quite competitive, and having a suspension of that sort on your record was not good. Thankfully, when I had gone through the three-day suspension, the supervising principal from the school district I had attended through ninth grade went to bat for me with the officials in the high school and requested that this infraction be taken off my record. That was an act of pure mercy and pure grace on the part of the supervising principal, and having the record of that suspension removed from my high school transcript helped me enormously in terms of my application for entrance to college. I still appreciate that.

But the cleansing of my record did not mean my guilt was erased. I got in the fight, so it was part of the ultimate record of my life. I broke the rule and I paid the price, but my guilt was not erased from reality. In much the same way, we can try, by many acts of penance, to make restitution for our violations of God's law. However, the guilt always remains.

So to ask the question, "What do you do with your guilt?" is simply to ask the question, "How do you live with yourself?" How do we live with our innate knowledge of what we have done and of who we are? We are objectively guilty in God's sight—and we must deal with that guilt.

The good news is that God has given us a way to deal with our guilt. In fact, we might say that the whole message of the Christian faith is the proclamation of God's solution to a problem we cannot solve ourselves. He has made a provision to deal with the reality of guilt, and He does it on the basis of real forgiveness, which is one of the most liberating, freeing, healing experiences of the human soul. That's the good news of the Christian message. In the next chapter, we'll look more closely at this good news.

Chapter Three

THE CURE—
FORGIVENESS

In the first year of my teaching career, when I was a professor at a college, a senior coed made an appointment to talk to me. I didn't know whether she wanted to talk about an academic problem, a personal issue, or something else, but when she came into my office, it was immediately clear that she was exceedingly distressed; in fact, she was so upset she could hardly talk. I asked her what her problem was, and she then related her story.

She was engaged to be married, and her wedding date was approaching rapidly. She was very happy in her anticipation of their marriage, but she was devastated by guilt feelings because of her relationship with her fiancé. She felt that way because the two of them had engaged in premarital sexual relations. Remember, this occurred prior to the sexual revolution, before that time in Western culture when premarital sex suddenly became culturally acceptable and even a badge of honor and sophistication among young people. This woman had not been influenced by that cultural transformation, and she was deeply, deeply concerned about her actions.

I asked her what she had done about her feelings of guilt. She told me that she had gone to the campus chaplain, had told him her story, and had told him that she felt guilty. He had been very kind, pastoral, and gentle toward her in his response. He said, "Do you love this man?" and she said that she did. He asked, "Are you planning to marry him?" and she told him they were engaged. Finally, he said to her, "Well, what you're doing with him is perfectly normal," and he cited statistics and studies that indicated the statistical normalcy of this kind of behavior.

Then he went on to say that she was feeling so guilty

because was the victim of a prudish culture. He told her she was living out the consequences of the Puritan era and the Victorian era, which held the conscience of America in a viselike grip. The chaplain informed this young woman that she simply needed to see that she was an adult and that she was expressing herself responsibly in her preparations for marriage. By having sexual relations, he said, she and her fiancé were finding out whether they were physically compatible. In essence, he told her she simply needed to grow up a little and have a mature view of her behavior, understanding that her guilt feelings had been imposed on her by the environment and the culture in which she lived.

After she told me this story, I asked her what had happened after this conversation. She said she still felt guilty. At that point, I said: "Well, maybe the reason you feel guilty is because you *are* guilty. You understand clearly that the law against premarital intercourse was not enacted first by the Puritans. Neither was sexual purity invented by Queen Victoria. God has commanded that you refrain from this kind of activity until you are in the sacred bonds of matrimony. You have violated the law of God."

I went on to tell her that I knew that the studies by

Alfred Kinsey and others had concluded that millions of other people also had broken that law, but I assured her that the fact that myriad people had broken the law did not annul the law. The law is based ultimately on God's own personal character. I told her that I knew parents often said, and maybe her parents had told her, not to engage in sex outside of marriage because of the risks of pregnancy, venereal disease, or social ostracism—all the deterrents that our culture put on people years ago. However, in the final analysis, I said, the reason to obey the law against sex outside of marriage is not merely to escape painful consequences but to avoid offending the holiness of God.

THE LAW OF GOD IS STILL VALID

At the time when I spoke with this woman, the cultural norms were generally opposed to sex outside of marriage. Today, the situation for young people is far worse. I'm well aware of how strong the physical urges can be and how strongly the culture bombards our senses with allurements and erotic enticements and stimulations. I think that this generation of young people has the biggest challenge to maintain chastity of any generation in American history.

They live in a culture that applauds illicit sexual behavior and they're stimulated sexually by every movie they see, every book they read, and the music they listen to. We need to bend over backward to be patient and understanding in terms of the severity of temptation that comes to young people today.

Still, while these factors may be mitigating circumstances in the sight of God, not one of them individually or all of them collectively have the force of annulling or repealing the law of God. The American Psychiatric Association does not make the rules for sexual purity. The Creator of man and woman has set forth His standards in His law, and He made sexual fidelity one of His top ten.

Many years ago, while doing some research in the field of apologetics, I was reading the writings of the first- and second-century Christian apologists, men such as Justin Martyr and others. One of the methods they used as they addressed the officials of the Roman Empire to argue for the truth claims of Christianity was an appeal to the sexual behavior of Christians. In the empire at that time, sexual expression was the norm. The apologists invited the Roman officials to inspect their families and communities, promising that they would find an extraordinary commitment to sexual purity. As an apologist in the twenty-first century, I wouldn't think of inviting that kind of scrutiny of the church as proof of Christianity, because the new morality has invaded the Christian community almost as deeply as it has the secular community.

In the early years of my ministry, one of the things that we had to deal with in the church was the problem of marriages that were falling apart. In marriage counseling, the number one problem that we had to work through was sexual conflict between the spouses. I can remember listening to husbands who were very upset because they claimed that their wives were sexually unresponsive or frigid. At that point, I began to ask those husbands a certain question: "Did you have sexual relations with your wife before your marriage?" I don't know how many times I asked married men that question, but I have to tell you that every single time I asked it, the answer was "Yes."

At that point, I would ask them a second question: "In your judgment, was your wife more responsive to you sexually before you were married or after you were married?" Every single time I asked that question, the men looked at me as if I were reading their minds. They would answer, "Before we were married."

At that point, I would tell those men that they might have a rose-colored view of the good old days, that their memories might not be quite accurate, or that it might have been the novelty of the relationship, the excitement of violating a taboo, that made their premarital sex seem so much more thrilling. But if their assessments were accurate and their wives were in fact less responsive physically since their weddings, perhaps it was because their wives had come into their marriage relationships with guilt that was not resolved. Perhaps, deep down, those women resented their husbands for causing them to compromise their integrity. Perhaps the sheer force of the guilt had paralyzed them, making it impossible for them to be free in their physical expressions. My point is this—in those experiences of counseling, there is no question that we were dealing time after time with a paralysis that was rooted and grounded in unresolved guilt.

THE POWER OF FORGIVENESS

Years ago, I did a teaching series on sex and single Christian women. In it I gave a series of lectures on sexual purity for women. The series was recorded and distributed, and it turned out to be one of the most popular series I ever did. I got literally hundreds of letters from people. Some were very critical, asking who I thought I was to teach such an outmoded view of ethics in this day and age. But most of the letters were from people for whom the lectures had hit a very vulnerable point in their lives. In the series, I said that in the sight of God, a man or a woman who has broken the law of God with respect to sexual purity can become a virgin again. That's the glory of the gospel. Jesus could go to Mary Magdalene, who was a prostitute, and could cleanse her and give her back her purity, virginity, and femininity. That's the power of forgiveness, for what happens in forgiveness, according to the Scriptures, is renewal.

I had a vivid experience of this early in my ministry. I was on staff in a church, and we had a special series of preaching services. I took my daughter, who was seven or eight years old at the time, to the church one evening during those services and dropped her off in the child-care center of the church, because the service that was being held was for adults. The visiting minister preached that night on the cross of Christ, and at the end he gave an invitation to the congregation, urging anyone who wanted to become a Christian to come forward. I was standing on the platform assisting in the service, and

I saw a multitude of people rushing toward the front of the sanctuary. To my utter shock, I saw my daughter coming forward. I had no idea what she was doing or even why she was in the sanctuary. My first thought was that I didn't want her coming forward in response to an emotional appeal when she was not ready to take seriously the claims of Christianity. I was kicking against the ox goad, as it were, watching my own daughter come forward to make a profession of faith in Christ. I really was concerned about it. I really was afraid that she was too young and didn't know what she was doing.

After the service, as we were on the way home, I said, "Well, Honey, why did you do that?" She said: "Daddy, I couldn't *not* do it. At first I thought I'd be too embarrassed to go forward, but I just couldn't stay in that seat. I had to go up there." I asked her, "Well, how do you feel now?" She said: "I feel clean. I feel like I've been washed, and I feel as fresh as a newborn baby." After I heard that, I said to myself, "I feel as dumb as they come." To this day, my daughter is a committed Christian. As a young child, she experienced the healing, renewing power of forgiveness.

In the end, it was the power of forgiveness that I shared with the young woman who came to me for counseling. I said: "You've told me what you've done. God's answer is not to paint a big red 'A' on your chest and make you walk through the community in shame and embarrassment, like the woman whom the Pharisees caught in adultery. The answer to guilt is always forgiveness. The only thing I know of that can cure real guilt is real forgiveness." I went on to say: "You've confessed your sin to me, and that's fine. I can tell you, 'God bless you.' But what you need to do is get by yourself, get down on your knees, and tell God what you have done. Tell Him that you're sorry and ask Him to forgive you and to make you clean."

That woman left my office skipping. Like Christian in *The Pilgrim's Progress*, the weight of iniquity rolled from her back because, as she prayed to God and confessed her sin, she experienced the forgiveness of Christ, not just in a symbolic sense but in a real way. In a very real sense, this woman went home a virgin. I believe many future problems with her husband were resolved that day.

FORGIVENESS AND FEELINGS OF FORGIVENESS

In the first chapter, I labored the point that there is an important difference between guilt and guilt feelings. The distinction is between that which is objective and that which is subjective. Guilt is objective; it is determined by a real analysis of what a person has done with respect to law. When a person transgresses a law, that person incurs guilt. This is true in the ultimate sense with regard to the law of God. Whenever we break the law of God, we incur objective guilt. We may deny that the guilt is there. We may seek to excuse it or deal with it in other ways, as we discussed in the previous chapter. Still, the reality is that we have the guilt.

However, guilt feelings may or may not correspond proportionately to one's objective guilt. In fact, in most cases, if not all cases, they *do not* correspond proportionately. As painful as guilt feelings can be—and we've all experienced the rigors of unsettling guilt feelings—I don't think any of us have ever experienced feelings of guilt in direct proportion to the actual guilt that we bear before God. I believe it is one of the mercies of God that He protects us from having to feel the full weight of the guilt that we actually have incurred in His sight.

Just as there are objective and subjective aspects of guilt, so there are objective and subjective aspects of forgiveness. First of all, forgiveness itself is objective. The only cure for real guilt is real forgiveness based on real repentance and real faith. However, we may have real and true forgiveness before God and yet not feel forgiven. Likewise, we may feel forgiven when we are not forgiven. That makes the issue of forgiveness very sticky.

We tend to trust our feelings to tell us what state we are in before God. Someone recently told me about a friend of hers who lives her Christian life on the basis of experience. I think that's a very dangerous thing, because it's like saying, "I determine truth by my subjective responses and feelings to it." I would much prefer that her friend tried to live the Christian life on the basis of Scripture, because Scripture is objective truth that transcends the immediacy of a person's experience.

CONFESSION BRINGS FORGIVENESS

Ultimately, the only source of real forgiveness is God. Thankfully, God is quick to forgive. In fact, one of the few absolute promises that God makes to us is that, if we confess our sins to Him, He will most seriously and surely forgive those sins (1 John 1:9).

Many years ago, I went to see my pastor to tell him about a struggle I was having with guilt. After I told him my problem, he opened the Bible to 1 John 1:8 and asked me to read this verse out loud. It says, "If we say we have no sin, we deceive ourselves, and the truth is not in us." In this verse, the apostle John is addressing the scenario we discussed earlier, in which a person who has real guilt attempts to deny or excuse it. John is saying that if we deny our guilt, we are simply fooling ourselves. We all sin. Therefore, we all contract guilt. If we refuse to accept that, we are engaged in perhaps the worst kind of deception, namely, self-deception. But when I read that passage, my pastor said to me: "That's not your problem, because you've just told me why you came here. You came to tell me that you had a problem with sin."

Then he had me read the next verse: "If we confess our sins, he is faithful and just to forgive us our sins and to cleanse us from all unrighteousness." When I finished reading that, he asked me, "Have you confessed your sin?" I said: "Yes. But I still feel guilty." He said: "OK. How about reading 1 John 1:9 for me." I looked at him in confusion and said, "That's what just I read." He said: "I know. I want you to read it again." So I picked up the Bible and I read, "If we confess our sins, he is faithful and just to forgive our sins and to cleanse us from all unrighteousness." Then

I looked up at the minister, and he said, "So, what else?" I said: "Well, I've read this passage, I understand what it is saying, and I've confessed my sin. But I still feel guilty." He said, "OK, this time I'd like you to read 1 John 1:9." He made me read it again, and I ended up reading it five or six times. Finally, he got my attention. He said, "R. C., here's what the truth of God declares: If 'A,' 'B' necessarily follows. God has promised that if you confess your sins, He will forgive you of your sins and cleanse you of your unrighteousness. You don't believe that you're forgiven because you don't feel forgiven. What, then, are you trusting—your feelings or the truth of God?" I finally got the message he was trying to help me see.

THE SIN OF ARROGANCE

I remembered that lesson years later when I was in the pastorate and had a similar experience. A woman came to me, just as I had gone to my pastor years before, and told me that she was guilty of a particular sin and she was plagued by a guilty conscience. So I did the same thing my pastor had done with me. I had her read 1 John 1:9. She read it, then said: "Well, I have confessed this sin and I have asked

God to forgive me of this sin a hundred times, but I still feel guilty. What can I do?" I said: "Well, let me ask you to do something else. I think you need to get on your knees and ask God to forgive you again."

When she heard that, she became very frustrated. She said: "You're supposed to be a theologian. I expected something a little more profound than this kind of advice from you. I've already told you that I have confessed this sin to God and asked Him to forgive me a hundred times." I told her: "I'm not asking you to confess *that* sin to God. I want you to confess a different sin." She asked, "What's that?" I replied, "I want you to confess your sin of arrogance." That really irritated her. She said: "Arrogance? What do you mean? I've been the most humble person in the world. I've been beating my breast and I've been on my face begging God to forgive me." So I said, "Does God say that if you confess He will forgive?" She answered, "Yes." So I said: "So how many times do you have to confess your sin to God? If you confess it once and truly repent of it, what does God say He will do?" She said, "He'll forgive it."

With that, I said to her: "But that wasn't good enough for you. You went to God a second time and said: 'Run that by me again. I don't really trust Your sincerity. I don't really believe, God, that You mean what You say when You promise that You will forgive me.' Or maybe what you're thinking is that the free remission of sins that God offers to humbly penitent people may be good enough for gross sinners but not for you. You're thinking: 'It can't be this easy. Let other people bask in mercy and grace. I have more dignity than that. I want to do something to make up for it.' But you can't make up for it. You're a debtor who can't pay your debts. All you can do is cry unto God, 'Lord, be merciful to me, a sinner,' and take God at His word. You have to live not by your feelings but by His truth. Your feelings are subjective, ephemeral. His Word is objective. It is true. If God says, 'I forgive you,' you are forgiven no matter how you feel, and to refuse that forgiveness is an act of arrogance."

Well, when she calmed down and listened to that explanation, she finally got the message. She said: "I see. I have been unwilling to forgive myself and unwilling to believe the Word of God because of my feelings."

THE DEVIL'S ACCUSATIONS

But I thought there was another aspect of the problem she needed to see, so I asked her, "Do you believe in Satan?"

I know that we live in a time and in a culture that has an almost totally secular worldview. It has no room for supernatural beings, but the Scriptures take Satan very seriously. The image of Satan in the New Testament is of one who goes about as a roaring lion seeking whom he can devour (1 Peter 5:8). The typical biblical imagery of a lion is that of a ferocious beast whose strength far transcends our own.

Christians tend to think that the work of Satan in their lives is focused or concentrated chiefly on temptation, because we meet Satan first in the form of a serpent in the Garden of Eden as he brings the temptation before Eve (Gen. 3). We see him again when Christ undergoes His testing period of forty days in the wilderness, when Satan appears to Him and seeks to seduce Him with temptation (Matt. 4). But we need to understand that while Satan does indeed tempt Christians, his primary work in the lives of believers is accusation. That's his favorite pastime. His very name means "slanderer."

As Christians, we know that the only way we can stand before God is by resting in His grace and on the finished work of Christ, by finding security in God's word of forgiveness. But Satan comes to believers, just as he came to Joshua the high priest in the book of Zechariah (Zech.

3:1–5), calling attention to our dirty garments and accusing us of our sins. Why does he do that? Why would Satan invest so much time and energy in accusing people who have been forgiven of their sins? As the archenemy of God and His church, Satan wants to paralyze us, to rob us of our freedom, to take away from us our joy and our delight in the free grace of God.

CONVICTION OR ACCUSATION?

The difficulty lies in the fact that God the Holy Spirit convicts us of sin, whereas Satan accuses us of sin. The same sin may produce both conviction and accusation. How, then, can we know, when we are being distressed or disturbed with feelings of guilt, whether the author of that distress is the Spirit of God or the Enemy?

Here is one way: When the Holy Spirit convicts us of sin, He does so to bring us to repentance and, ultimately, to bring us to reconciliation with God, to forgiveness, to healing, and to cleansing. In other words, when the Spirit of God convicts us of sin, His entire purpose and entire motive is redemptive. When Satan accuses us, perhaps of the same sin, his purpose is to destroy us. That's why Paul says: "Who shall bring any charge against God's elect? It is God who justifies. Who is to condemn?" (Rom. 8:33–34a). He then becomes rhapsodic and says:

Who shall separate us from the love of Christ? Shall tribulation, or distress, or persecution, or famine, or nakedness, or danger, or sword? As it is written, "For your sake we are being killed all the day long; we are regarded as sheep to be slaughtered." No, in all these things we are more than conquerors through him who loved us. For I am sure that neither death nor life, nor angels nor rulers, nor things present nor things to come, nor powers, nor height nor depth, nor anything else in all creation, will be able to separate us from the love of God in Christ Jesus our Lord. (vv. 35–39)

So, the way to silence the Accuser is to confess our sins before God and believe the Word of God, even as Jesus did in His temptation experience. He sent Satan away by rejecting his advances with the truth of God. The Bible says, "Resist the devil, and he will flee from you" (James 4:7b). The power of resistance that we have is the truth of

God. How can we better resist the accusation of a guilty conscience than to say to Satan, "I have confessed that sin to God and He has forgiven me"? If we resist him in that way, we will see the roaring lion running down the street with his tail between his legs.

Yes, there is a thin line of distinction between conviction and accusation, and it takes wisdom, persistence, and saturation in the truth of God to discern the difference.

When it comes to our guilt before God, we must say with David, "If you, O LORD, should mark iniquities, O Lord, who could stand?" (Ps. 130:3). I couldn't stand. You couldn't stand. The only support system we have for standing in the presence of God as sinners who have violated the law of God is the forgiveness that God gives us in Jesus Christ. We need real forgiveness. If feelings of forgiveness come with it, that's a bonus, but we cannot live on the basis of our feelings. The gospel is not addressed to sensuous spirituality, but to trust in the objective truth of God.

But that real forgiveness requires real repentance and real faith, and without real repentance and real faith there is no real forgiveness to real guilt before God. Our guilt should drive us to search for the way of forgiveness and reconciliation that God provides for His people; it should drive us to the cross, where Christ paid the price for our transgressions.

The simple truth is that if God forgives us, we are forgiven. That's an objective state of affairs. Maybe our friends will not forgive us. Maybe our spouses will not forgive us. Maybe society will not forgive us. Maybe the government will not forgive us. But if God forgives us, we are forgiven. That doesn't mean that we were never guilty. We cannot have forgiveness without real guilt. But forgiveness releases us from the punishment that we justly deserve because of our guilt. Through it, we can be restored to a healthy and loving relationship with God.

About the Author

Dr. R.C. Sproul is the founder and chairman of Ligonier Ministries, an international Christian discipleship organization located near Orlando, Fla. He also serves as copastor at Saint Andrew's Chapel in Sanford, Fla., as chancellor of Reformation Bible College, and as executive editor of *Tabletalk* magazine. His teaching can be heard around the world on the daily radio program *Renewing Your Mind*.

During his distinguished academic career, Dr. Sproul helped train men for the ministry as a professor at several theological seminaries.

He is author of more than ninety books, including *The Holiness of God*, *Chosen by God*, *The Invisible Hand*, *Faith Alone*, *Everyone's a Theologian*, *Truths We Confess*, *The Truth of the Cross*, and *The Prayer of the Lord*. He also served as general editor of the *Reformation Study Bible* and has written several children's books, including *The Donkey Who Carried a King*. Dr. Sproul and his wife, Vesta, make their home in Sanford, Fla.

Further your Bible study with *Tabletalk* magazine, another learning tool from R.C. Sproul.

....

TABLETALK MAGAZINE FEATURES:

- A Bible study for each day—bringing the best in biblical scholarship together with down-to-earth writing, *Tabletalk* helps you understand the Bible and apply it to daily living.

- Trusted theological resource—*Tabletalk* avoids trends, shallow doctrine and popular movements to present biblical truth simply and clearly.

- Thought-provoking topics—each issue contains challenging, stimulating articles on a wide variety of topics related to theology and Christian living.

Sign up for a free 3-month trial of *Tabletalk* magazine and we will send you R.C. Sproul's *The Holiness of God*

TryTabletalk.com/CQ